The Best of

Grandma's

Compiled by Mr

Young Learner Publications™
G-1, Rattan Jyoti,
18, Rajendra Place,
New Delhi -110008 (INDIA)
Ph.: 25750801, 25820556
Fax: 91-11-25764396

Printed at : Kumar Offset Printers, Delhi-110092

CONTENTS

THE FREE BLUEBIRD

A bluebird sat on the ledge of an open window of a very big house.

She looked inside the house and saw a parrot in a cage.

The parrot said, "Why are you peeping inside, Bluebird? Are you jealous of me?"

The bluebird said, “No dear Parrot. I am not jealous. I was just pitying you because you are enclosed in a cage.”

“Don’t pity me. I get good food to eat without having to search for it,” said the parrot proudly.

The bluebird said, “But you cannot experience the pleasure of being free and flying up in the blue sky.”

“Here people call me ‘beautiful’ and play with me,” said the parrot proudly.

“When the children see me, they call out, ‘Good Luck’. I love that,” said the bluebird.

“My cage is very expensive and can you see this gold band on my neck? It is very costly,” said the parrot.

“I would not exchange my freedom to fly in the sky for anything, not even all the gold or diamonds of the world,” said the bluebird happily.

The parrot said, “In a cage I have nothing to fear. I am safe from eagles and vultures.”

The bluebird said, "You are right, dear Parrot. There is a lot of danger out in the sky."

Just then a boy came over with a knitting needle and started poking the parrot with it.

The parrot was getting hurt by the pointed knitting needle and he started flapping his wings.

He said sadly, "You were right, Bluebird. If I had been out of this cage, I could have flown away from this bad boy."

The bluebird felt very bad that the boy was hurting the parrot.

The bluebird became angry with the boy for being so cruel and unkind.

The bluebird started shouting loudly, “Screech. Trrrrr. Screech. Leave the parrot. Don’t hurt him. I will hit you. You are a bad boy. Stop it!”

The boy heard the bluebird and ran towards him. The boy tried to poke the bluebird also with the needle.

The bluebird moved away from the needle and bit the boy hard on his hand. Then he flew away to safety but the boy kept crying, nursing his injured hand.

HONEY STUCK

The father, the mother and their twin daughters, Sue and Annie lived together happily.

The twin daughters, one day saw that their father and mother were very worried and sad.

Sue asked, "What is the matter, Mother? Why are you worried?"

The mother said, "The village landlord wants us to vacate this house."

Annie said, "But this is our house. It is in the name of Father."

"The landlord says that this house belongs to him," replied the mother sadly.

"Father, who is in the right in this case?" asked Annie.

"You know Annie that I never cheat. My grandfather had bought this house with his hard earned money, and my father lived here all his life," said father.

"So, is he cheating us?" asked Sue.

"Yes, Sue. Had the house belonged to the landlord, I would have surely vacated it," replied father.

The next morning, the village landlord came with some bad men and said, "It has been decided that on Monday the lawyers and the police will come. Before that you have to handover the keys of the house to me. If you do not leave the house and go away, my men will kill you all."

After the landlord had gone away with his men, the father said, "Let us pack our things and leave the house. He will not let us stay here anymore."

Sue said, "No, Father. This is our house and some bad people cannot make us leave it. We love this house and shall always live here. No one can make us vacate our own house."

"But what can we do?" asked the father.

The twins talked for some time and then Sue said, "Just get a lot of honey and cottonwool."

The father trusted his daughters and he bought a lot of honey and cottonwool.

They had three very small rooms, side by side in their house. In one room Sue and Annie spread all the honey and in the other they put all the cottonwool.

On the day the lawyers had to come, the landlord came with his bad men and told them to wait outside the house.

He wanted to go into the house but he found all the doors locked. Only one door was open.

He opened the door and went in the room filled with honey. He rushed in and in doing so slipped on the honey covered ground.

He fell down with a loud thud. Cursing the people of the house, he got up with great difficulty for he kept slipping on the honey.

Grumbling and fuming with anger, he went to the next room and found it to be full of cottonwool, which stuck to the sticky honey all over his body.

Meanwhile, the landlord's lawyer, the people from the court and the police were waiting outside the house.

His lawyer told his men, "Call the landlord. If he is not here, then he shall have no claim on the house. Then he cannot ask this family to move out."

Some of the landlord's men said, "This family has kidnapped our master. He went inside the house sometime back and hasn't come out."

Sue said, "We didn't see anybody. Nobody has come here and if he doesn't come for another ten minutes, then this house is ours."

The men quickly started looking for their master. As the girls had bolted the front door, they tried the other doors.

They finally entered the room with the honey and then ran to the room with the cottonwool, just like the landlord.

Then they screamed as they saw a furry creature, who angrily said, "Hush. I am the landlord."

They shouted, "Master! You look funny, but go out at once or you will lose the house. Hurry up."

And they opened the other door that led to the front room and pushed the landlord out. All the people were shocked to see a huge mass of cottonwool walk out of the house.

It looked like a furry, white animal and everyone laughed.

The furry animal shouted, "I am the landlord. I have come. This house is mine."

The police officer said, "No. You are wrong. This house rightfully belongs to this family. We have seen the papers thoroughly. You are in the wrong."

Just then all the bad men also came out, covered all over with sticky cottonwool.

Everyone was now laughing at them and the landlord shouted at Sue, "Stop laughing. You have cheated me by putting all that honey and cotton wool in the rooms."

"But we did not invite you inside," said Annie.

"It was wrong of you to go into their house before we came, so now come with us to the police station," said the police officer.

The landlord and the bad men were taken to the police station and the family lived happily in that house.

THE DOG AND THE BONE

A dog was roaming around, looking for food. He did not find anything to eat, so he sat down sadly in front of a butcher's shop.

The butcher saw him and taking pity on the dog, threw a bone at him.

The dog quickly jumped and caught the bone in his mouth. The dog was very happy but he saw that the other dogs had seen the bone. The dog was afraid that the other dogs would take it.

So with the bone tightly held in his mouth, he quickly ran away. He decided to run far away and eat it alone.

But the other dogs came after him. The dog then thought that he would cross the river.

The river had a small bridge, which was quite low.

The dog started walking on that bridge. Then he looked back and was happy that the other dogs were not following him.

Suddenly he saw another dog. The dog was down below the bridge, in the water.

The dog growled angrily, "grrrrrr, gggrrrh, gggrrrrrrr," because he thought that the other dog in the water would take his bone.

But then he saw that the other dog already had a bone. And the other bone seemed to be bigger than his bone.

"I must take the bigger bone from this other dog," thought the dog.

“Gggrrrr, Gggrrr, give me the bone,” growled the dog.

As he opened his mouth, the bone fell into the water. The dog got very angry.

The dog barked loudly and jumped into the water to take the bone.

The water of the stream was very cold and to his utter surprise he did not find any other dog in the water.

The water of the stream was also very fast and the foolish dog nearly drowned in the water.

He tried to save himself by swimming in the water. After a lot of labour he could finally get out of the water.

Then he sat thinking, "What a fool I have been! There was no other dog in the water. I was just seeing my own reflection in the water. This serves me right. I have lost the bone which I had just because I wanted a bigger bone. Now I will have to remain hungry till I find something else to eat."

THE HELPFUL CROW

The crow saw the peacock dancing and really liked him.

"You are very beautiful," said the crow to the peacock.

The peacock looked at the crow and said, "But you are ugly and black. I don't want to talk to you at all."

The crow said, "Why are you being so rude, Peacock?"

"I will do what I want. You keep quiet," said the peacock.

The crow said, "I may be black but I am not bad at heart."

The peacock just walked away. The crow felt very bad but did not say anything.

A pigeon had heard the proud peacock talking rudely to the crow.

She had not liked the way the peacock had called the crow 'ugly and black'.

The pigeon said to the crow, "This peacock looks so beautiful outside, but he is so rude."

The crow said to the pigeon, "It doesn't matter. Let it be."

The crow flew to his nest. He had no family; so he lived alone. As he had eaten his food, he went to sleep.

The next morning he woke up to the sound of the two tiny babies of the peacock playing under his tree. The crow flew off to find food for himself.

The peacock and his wife, the peahen always walked around to gather food for their children.

That day they could not find anything to eat, so they had to go far into the forest. All the birds had gone to get food for their babies.

When the crow came back, he saw that the two children of the peacock were still under his tree.

He sat down and just kept watching them. Suddenly he felt that something was wrong.

He looked around. There was no other bird around. All the children were in their nests where their parents had left them.

The crow still felt that something bad was going to happen. So he became alert.

All of a sudden, an eagle attacked the baby peacocks.

The crow was ready. He flew straight at the eagle, who himself was taken by surprise when the crow attacked him.

The eagle flew off. The baby peacocks ran away crying with fear.

The eagle attacked again. This time too the crow was ready and it attacked the eagle.

The crow and the eagle fought a fierce battle. The crow was trying to save the small baby peacocks with all his might.

The eagle flew off and the crow came back to his tree.

He looked around but could not see the baby peacock anywhere. Just a few of their feathers lay scattered on the ground below.

"Have the babies been hurt? Oh! I could not save them," thought the sad crow.

Then he saw them. They were hiding under a bush. They did not appear to be hurt, just scared.

Just then the peacock came. He was frightened when he saw that his babies were not there.

The peacock looked up to see that the crow was the only one there and that he had blood on his beak.

The peacock was very angry. He shouted at the crow, "Where are my children? I am sure you have eaten them."

The crow was too shocked to reply. The peacock went on saying, “I was right about you. You are black and your heart too is black.”

The babies heard the voice of their father and quickly came out from under the bush.

One of the babies said, “Father, don’t be angry with him. Uncle Crow saved us.”

The babies then told their father about the attack of the eagle. The peacock felt ashamed of himself.

He apologised to the crow, “I am sorry. I shouted at you not realising that you had saved my children.”

The crow said, “It is all right. You must have been worried about your children.”

The peacock said, “I was worried but it was wrong of me to shout at you. You saved my babies but I thought that you had killed them. I should not have shouted at you without finding out the truth.”

Just then the peahen came and said, “Please pardon us. Thank you very much for saving our children. Can we all be friends now?”

The crow said, “Yes, of course.”

The peacock and his family then became very friendly with the crow. They lived happily together. The crow was no longer lonely for now he had true friends.

TIT FOR TAT

There was a fox who was very clever and naughty. He always tried to tease other animals and birds.

One day, he saw a tall and lovely crane. The fox felt that he was very ugly as compared to the beautiful and tall crane.

He saw the long beak of the crane and then he got an idea. He could tease the crane and have fun.

The fox said, "Mr Crane, please come and have dinner at my place."

The crane agreed and that evening he went to the house of the fox for dinner.

The fox was very polite and he talked to the crane very nicely. The crane felt very happy.

Then the fox brought dinner. He said, "Mr Crane, I have prepared soup for you. Please have it and you are sure to like it."

The fox served the soup in a shallow soup plate.

The crane had such a long beak that he could not eat even a tiny bit of the soup.

The crane had come for dinner and was very hungry. He felt very bad.

"Oh Mr Crane! Isn't the soup delicious?" asked the clever fox, lapping up the soup.

The crane was quiet and the fox finished all the soup.

After finishing the soup, the fox asked, "Did you enjoy the soup, Mr. Crane?"

The crane just nodded his head. He was feeling very hungry because he had not been able to even taste the soup.

The crane thought that the fox would bring something more to eat but the fox said, "The soup was so good and filling that I am feeling sleepy."

The crane said, "Then I must take your leave Mr Fox, but first you must promise to come to my house for dinner tomorrow. I shall cook fish."

The fox agreed happily because he loved to eat fish.

Next morning he thought of the wonderful fish he would eat in the evening at the crane's house.

The fox went to the house of the crane. He could smell the fish being cooked and his mouth began to water.

Then the crane served the fish in two very tall jars.

He said, "Mr Fox, I have prepared a very delicious dish of fish. Please enjoy it."

The fox could only lick the top of the jar while the crane started eating the fish with his long beak.

Then the fox tried again because he was very hungry and in doing so, his snout got stuck in the jar.

The fox tried to take out his snout from the tall jar but it would not come out.

The crane said, “Isn’t the fish wonderful? Oh, I have cooked very well today.”

The poor fox could say nothing. He shook his head and then pulled hard. His snout then came out of the jar.

The crane said, “Oh Mr Fox! Have you enjoyed the dinner?”

The fox nodded his head and rubbed his snout because it was hurting where it had got stuck in the mouth of the jar.

Then the crane laughed and said, “Oh Mr Fox! Your snout has become so red. You are looking like a joker.”

The crane went on laughing for a long time, and the fox felt very bad.

The fox said, “Mr Crane, my snout got stuck in your tall jar. I could not eat the fish.”

The crane said, “Mr Fox, when you served soup in a shallow plate, I could not eat it either, so you should not be feeling bad now?”

The fox realised his mistake and said, “I am sorry for that. Now I promise I will never tease you, Mr Crane.”

THE SMART DOG

A wolf was very hungry. He had not found anything to eat. Then he saw a dog.

The dog was sitting under a tree. The wolf wanted to eat the dog, but then he thought that the dog was very thin.

He felt that the thin dog would have only bones and no flesh, so he would not be tasty.

But he was so hungry that he thought that he just had to eat the dog.

The wolf walked towards the dog and then the dog saw him and felt afraid.

The dog wanted to run away, but he knew that he could not run very fast. The wolf would catch him anyway.

The dog quickly thought, "I have to save myself from the wolf. There is no one else who can help me."

The dog thought of a plan and said, "Dear wolf, so you want to eat me?"

"Yes, I will eat you just now," growled the hungry wolf.

"I am ready to be eaten, dear wolf, but what will you get? I have just bones and no flesh on my body. Even my name is Thinny," said the dog.

"You are too thin, but I am very hungry," said the wolf.

"If only you could wait for sometime," said the clever dog.

"What do you mean?" asked the wolf.

The dog said, "My master's daughter is getting married today. He is organising a feast."

"So?" asked the wolf.

The dog said, "I will get a lot of things to eat. After eating all that, I would be fatter and there would be more flesh on me, so I would be more tasty."

The wolf thought, "What the dog is saying, is true. I will wait for a while and then eat him, but what if he runs away?"

The dog interrupted his thoughts and said, "Dear wolf, where should I meet you?"

Aloud the wolf said, "You can meet me wherever you want."

"Then after an hour, please come near that gate, because I will be so heavy after the feast, that I will not be able to walk far," said the thin dog.

As the wolf walked off, the thin dog ran straight to the huge dog, Biggy, who lived with him.

"What is the matter, why are you looking afraid, Thinny?" asked the huge dog.

"Oh Biggy! I just saved myself from a wolf who wanted to eat me," said Thinny.

He told Biggy whatever had happened with the wolf.

"Thinny, you have been very clever. Good, now let the wolf come here. I will have fun," said Biggy.

After an hour, the wolf came back to that gate.

He called, "Thinny, come here. I have come for you."

Thinny said, "Dear wolf, so you have come. I am behind this gate."

"Come out fast," said the wolf who was really very hungry now.

Thinny said, "I am ready to be eaten. I have become really fleshy. Just let me open the gate."

Slowly the gate opened and the wolf smiled to think of what a lovely meal he would have, when he would eat the fleshy Thinny.

Suddenly Biggy came out and rushed at the wolf, who was shocked. When the wolf saw how huge Biggy was, he ran away. Thinny was standing behind Biggy and they both burst out laughing.

The wolf never ever ventured near that gate again.

THE BROKEN FRIENDSHIP

A lion saw three bullocks standing together. He hid behind the tree and waited for a chance to eat them.

The three bullocks stayed together the whole day. Then in the evening, the lion was so hungry that he decided to attack them.

The three bullocks standing together, got alert when they saw the lion.

The lion saw how strong and pointed their horns were. He was so afraid that he ran away from there without attacking them.

Everyday the lion would sit and watch the three bullocks. They were fat and healthy and the lion wanted to eat them.

But he could not attack them because he was afraid of the three big bullocks.

The lion felt angry at the deep friendship between the bullocks.

He knew that he could kill and eat one bullock at a time but he could not kill all three together.

The lion was waiting for a chance to get one bullock away from the others and then kill him.

The thought of eating their juicy flesh made his mouth water. He longed for the day when he would be able to dig his claws in their juicy flesh.

One morning, the lion came as usual to see if the bullocks were together or not.

That day he smiled because he saw that the three bullocks were fighting.

The lion sat down to wait because now he knew that they would not stay together.

The three bullocks were angry and they fought for a long time. Then one bullock walked away and stood away from the other two in a corner.

The two bullocks who were together were quiet for some time, but then they too started fighting.

After a few minutes, one of them walked away from both to another corner.

Now all three were standing in three different corners of the field, like enemies.

The lion thought, "I love it when others fight. If they are together, then I can't eat them. But if they are alone, then I kill them one by one and enjoy their flesh."

The lion attacked the bullocks one by one and killed them. If only the bullocks had remained friends, the lion would not have succeeded in killing them!

THE FROG AND THE BOYS

A family of frogs had made their home near the bank of a river.

One morning, they all went into the river water to have a bath. They started swimming and having fun.

One frog said to another, "I feel so happy being together and playing without a care in the world?"

The other agreed but just then a stone fell near the frogs.

They looked up and saw some boys standing on the bank of the river.

One boy said, "I threw the stone so far in the water. I bet you can't throw it that far."

"Of course I can," said another boy.

The boys started having a competition. The frogs felt very afraid when the boys started throwing stones one after the other, into the river.

One after the other, stones kept falling in the river, some stones even hit the frogs.

A huge stone fell on the oldest frog's head who then cried to his family, "Run! Save yourself!"

The frogs tried to run away but the stones came very quickly and hit many of them.

The oldest frog said, “What are these boys doing? Don’t they know they are hurting us?”

His wife said, “Maybe they really don’t know that they are hurting us.”

“I must talk to them,” said the oldest frog.

“No. You might be hit by another stone,” said his wife.

“I can’t see my family being hurt like this,” said the oldest frog and he swam out of the water.

He quickly climbed onto a leaf and shouted, “Trrr, tarrr. Listen to me. Please don’t hit us.”

One boy told the other boys, “Stop. See that frog is trying to tell us something.”

All the boys stopped throwing stones. The frog said, “Please don’t throw stones.”

One boy said, "Don't stop us. We are having a competition, and a lot of fun."

"But we are getting hurt," said the frog.

"We are not hitting you. We are just throwing stones in the water," said the fourth boy.

"We get hurt when you throw the stones. My family is still inside the river," said the frog.

The first boy picked up a stone ready to throw it at the frog.

He shouted, "Hey froggie. Don't spoil our fun or we will hit you with a stone."

Mrs. Frog shouted to her husband, "Get away. These boys might kill you."

But the frog said, "Please boys, there are many fish in the river too. They can be hurt too by your stones. Be kind, please."

The first boy was about to throw a stone at the oldest frog but the second boy stopped him and said, "No. We will not throw stones in the water. For a bit of fun we cannot be cruel, and hurt so many creatures living in the water. How would we feel if someone hurts us for the mere sake of some fun?"

All the boys agreed, “Froggie, we are sorry. We did not know we were hurting you all. Now we won’t throw stones. So be happy and take care.”

All the frogs thanked the oldest frog for saving them. The four boys walked away and never threw stones again in the river.

THE MIGHTY SUN

The wind looked at the sun and asked, "Why does everyone call you great?"

The sun said, "They call me great because I am great."

"No, you are not great. I am greater than you," said the wind.

The sun said, "We both are necessary for people, but I am more important."

"People cannot live without air, so I am more important," said the wind.

"If I stop shining, everything will stop, even you," said the sun.

"I don't believe you. I am more powerful than you," argued the wind.

The sun laughed and said, "Let us have a competition to test ourselves. Can you see that man down there on earth?"

"Yes," said the wind, looking down on the earth where a man was standing, wearing a coat.

The sun said, “Well, let us see who is stronger. The one who gets him to take off his coat will be the winner.”

The wind agreed and the sun said, “Your chance first.”

The wind started blowing with all its power. The man pulled the coat closer around his body.

"You have made him clutch his coat closer. You have failed," said the sun.

The wind said, "I haven't finished yet."

The wind blew harder as in a storm and the man held his coat more tightly.

The sun said, "You could not make him remove the coat."

"All right. You try and see. Let's see if you can get him to remove the coat," said the wind.

The sun started smiling. He let his warm rays fall on the man. After a few moments the man felt warm.

The sun began to shine more brightly. The man let his coat loose as he felt the greater warmth of the sun.

Then the sun became stronger and stronger. The earth became hotter and hotter.

It became so hot that even the wind started feeling hot. The man on the earth started perspiring. He took out his handkerchief and wiped the sweat on his face.

Then some minutes later he removed his coat and went to sit under the shade of a tree.

As the wind kept quiet, the sun shouted with delight , "I have won!"

THE CUNNING FOX

A fox was walking in the forest. He decided to go to the nearby village to look for some food.

He walked around the village and then he saw a bullock. He wished he could eat the bullock.

As he was thinking about the bullock, he did not see what was in front of him.

There was a well and the fox fell into it. He tried hard to come out of the well but couldn't.

The wolf felt very helpless because he did not know how to get out of the well.

Thankfully there was very little water in the well, so the fox did not drown.

He stayed in the well trying to think of a way to get out.

Just then he heard someone coming to the well. The fox at once became alert.

He looked up to see the face of a goat looking into the well. He waited to see what the goat would do. The goat asked, "Do we have to go down there to drink water?"

The fox said, "Yes. That is the only way to drink water from this well."

The goat asked, "I am very thirsty. Is the water down there fit for drinking?"

The fox said, "Yes, it is wonderful. It is the sweetest water I have ever tasted. Come in."

The goat jumped into the well. In a flash of a second, the fox jumped on the goat's back.

The fox then leapt out of the well, leaving the goat inside. The goat looked around and saw that the water was dirty.

The goat said, "The water here is so muddy. I can't drink it. You have fooled me. You got me in and used me to jump out."

The fox replied, "Very true, you stupid goat."

The goat asked, "Why are you calling me stupid? You are bad and cunning."

The fox said, "I called you stupid because you trusted me. It is your mistake. Why did you believe me? Why didn't you see for yourself?"

The goat said, "Please help me out of the well."

But the fox had already run away leaving the poor goat in the well.

The goat thought, "I should not have acted without thinking."

STRENGTH OF UNITY

A man had four sons who were always fighting with each other. They would quarrel over anything and everything.

One day, the father bought a new bicycle for them, and they fought over that too. Their father was very, very upset with their behaviour.

The worried father thought for a while and then said to his wife, “Go and tell the children to come to me.” He could still hear his sons fighting and screaming over the bicycle.

His wife went outside to call the children, but they were too busy shouting at each other. They were screaming and hitting each other.

The mother went and told her husband what she had seen outside.

The father then went outside the house. He collected some sticks and brought them inside.

His wife came and asked him, “Why are you collecting these sticks? Are you going to beat the boys?”

Her husband said, “Just wait and watch.”

The father went out to the children and shouted at them to keep quiet. He looked sternly towards the boys. They had never before seen their father so angry. The father asked them to step closer to him.

Seeing the sticks in their father's hands, they got scared and without another word, went up to him. They came and stood next to their father.

The father tied four sticks with a rope and giving them to his eldest son, said, "I want you to break these sticks without untying them."

The eldest son tried and tried but could not break them. The father then passed on the bundle of sticks to his other sons. They all tried hard but none could break the sticks.

Then the father separated the sticks and gave one to each of them. He said, "Now break the sticks."

The sticks broke easily. The father said, "When I gave you all the sticks together, then you all could not break them. It means that if you remain together, then others cannot defeat you."

The sons stood listening quietly as their father continued, "But when I gave you one stick each, then you could break it easily."

“This mean that if you fight amongst yourselves, then others will take advantage. So my dear sons, you should love each other and stop fighting. Unity makes you strong,” he added as the boys stood silently, listening to what their father was saying.

They were beginning to realise that what their father was saying, was true indeed.

The mother added, “We love you, so we want you all to be happy and together.”

The eldest son said to his parents, “You both are right. We were being stupid and naughty. Now we will be good and stop fighting. We will always be together from now onwards.”

The sons stopped fighting from that day and lived together in peace and harmony. They learnt not to be selfish but caring and affectionate towards each other.

Their parents were indeed happy and relieved to see their sons sharing their toys and living together happily.

THE MONKEY KING

All the animals of the forest were sick and tired of the cruel lion king, who dictated his terms on all the animals.

The animals had a meeting to choose a new ruler. All of a sudden the monkey got up and started dancing.

The naughty monkey made funny movements and all the animals laughed.

The monkey jumped, moved his hips, rolled over and made funny faces and all the animals enjoyed it a lot.

They were so happy with the dance of the monkey that they made him their new king.

The monkey was very happy. He got up and danced again and all the animals clapped and cheered.

Only the fox was very angry. He had thought that all the animals would make him the king because he was so clever.

The fox thought that the monkey was just a clown and would not be able to rule properly.

He thought of teaching the monkey a lesson.

One day the fox ran to the monkey and said, "I have found some wonderful things to eat. I did not eat them, because as the king, you should get everything first."

The monkey was very happy and went with the fox. He saw some food. Without thinking, he quickly reached out for the food but got caught in a net laid by the fox.

The monkey realised that the fox had trapped him and now he was laughing at him.

The fox said, “Ha! Ha! You have been made the king and you cannot even look after yourself.”

“You tricked me,” said the monkey.

The fox said, "A king should be able to take care of himself. You are not fit to be the king."

Meanwhile, all the other animals had also gathered there. The clever fox narrated the entire incident to the animals.

The elephant said, "Yes this monkey is not fit to be the king."

The giraffe said, "We must have another meeting and choose a new ruler."

The monkey was taken out from the net but the crown was taken from him. He was no longer the king.

All the animals got together again for another meeting to choose another king.

THE RACE

The hare laughed at the tortoise and said, "You are so slow. Look at me, I can run so fast."

"Don't laugh at me," said the tortoise, feeling really bad.

"I bet if someone invites you today, you will reach his house tomorrow," laughed the hare.

"Certainly not! I am not that slow. If you want to see, then let us have a race," said the tortoise.

"You want to race me! What a joke! Ha! Ha! I will win very easily," said the hare confidently.

"We will see. First let us have the race, if you are not afraid to lose," said the tortoise.

"Poof! Why will I be afraid of losing? You should be the one to be afraid, you slow coach. So let us have a race," said the hare proudly.

Then they both stood waiting for someone to come by and judge their race.

A fox happened to cross their way. The tortoise and the hare stopped him to witness the race. The fox agreed and marked the beginning point. He then went and stood at the finishing point.

No sooner had the fox signalled the start of the race than the hare took off with big leaps. He was well ahead of the tortoise.

After a while, the hare thought, "I am feeling tired. Let me take a nap for some time because the tortoise is really slow."

The hare went to sleep but the tortoise walked on and on.

The tortoise did not rest even for a moment. He walked on as fast as he could, while the hare slept.

The hare woke up with a start. He looked behind him but could not see the tortoise.

He looked in front and he saw the tortoise nearing the finishing line. He cried, "Oh! What have I done? I have overslept and the tortoise is almost winning."

The hare ran as fast as he could, but the tortoise reached the finishing line before the hare.

The fox held up one hand of the tortoise and shouted, “The tortoise is the winner of this race. The stupid hare is the loser.”

The hare reached there and said, “Yes, foxy. I am very stupid. I had become too proud of myself. I went off to sleep because I was overconfident.”

The tortoise said, “Don’t feel bad about losing, dear hare. You are faster than me.”

“I am not feeling bad about losing to you, but I am feeling angry with myself. I was so careless that I went to sleep,” said the hare sadly.

The fox said, “I must congratulate you, dear tortoise. You deserved to win today.”

THE PEACOCK RAVEN

The raven thought, "I am black. I don't even have the white band on the neck that crows have. I don't like myself."

He looked at the other birds. He thought, "Just look at the other birds. That parrot is so pretty with its green feathers."

Sadly and slowly he walked to the lake. There he saw the beautiful white swans, so graceful and so lovely. He was even more upset now.

Then he saw a peacock and he thought, "Peacocks are the most beautiful. What lovely colours they have! I wish I was like them. Why can't I be as beautiful as the peacock?"

The raven flew to the middle of the forest where the peacocks lived.

The peacocks did not like the raven.

One peacock said to his friend, "Let us go away from here. This black raven is so ugly."

The raven felt bad but he didn't say anything.

He quickly picked up all the feathers of the peacocks that had fallen down.

The raven stuck the feathers on his tail and told other ravens, “See I have become more beautiful than you all.”

He teased the other ravens and said that they all were ugly.

The others said, "You cannot change yourself just by covering yourself with peacock feathers. You will always be a raven."

The raven felt that the other ravens were foolish and so he went to the peacocks trying to show off his new feathers.

But the peacocks looked at him and said, "Go away from here. You are not a peacock."

"But I am covered with your feathers," said the raven.

"Covering yourself with our feathers will not make you like us. Just get out of here," shouted the peacocks.

The peacocks threw out the raven. He felt very bad. Slowly he went back to his ravens.

But now the ravens said, "You made fun of us because you thought you looked as beautiful as the peacocks. Why have you come back here? Get out of here."

The raven now had to live alone. He thought, "I should have been happy with what I was. Why did I do all this? Now I will never be proud. I will have to live alone. No one will ever be my friend."

THE CLEVER ASS

An ass was grazing in a field which was near a forest. The ass suddenly felt as if someone was watching him.

He looked up but could see no one there. He started eating grass again. But he felt uneasy.

He looked carefully and saw a wolf hiding behind a tree in the forest. The wolf was watching him.

The ass felt afraid because he knew that the wolf could attack him. He looked around but there was no one.

The ass thought, "There is no one to help me. I have to save myself. I must think of a plan."

The ass saw the wolf coming out of the forest and walking towards him.

The ass thought, "Now I am in real danger. I must think of something very quickly. I must not become the meal for this ferocious looking wolf. Oh! God, please help. What should I do?"

As the wolf came nearer, the ass started walking with a limp, as if he was lame.

The wolf asked, "What is the matter? Why are you limping?"

"There is a thorn in my foot. Please take it out," said the ass.

"Why should I take it out?" asked the wolf.

The ass said, "Mr Wolf, I know you will eat me but if I have a thorn in my foot, it might hurt you."

"How will it hurt me?" asked the wolf.

"The thorn can hurt your throat when you eat me," said the clever ass.

"You are right. I don't want to choke on the thorn," said the wolf.

"So please take out the thorn from my foot. I don't want you to get hurt," said the ass.

The wolf said, "All right. Just lift your foot a bit and I will take out the thorn."

The ass raised his foot and the wolf started looking for the thorn which was not there.

All of a sudden, the ass kicked the wolf with his foot and the wolf fell down.

When the wolf got up, he looked for the ass but there was no one around because the ass had run away.

The wolf said, "I thought that asses were foolish, but even an ass can be clever."

THE WOLF AND THE KID

All the goats were going together to a field to eat grass. The older goats were looking after the young ones.

One mother goat said to her baby goat, "Kid, walk in the centre or you may get lost."

The baby goat said, "Mother, you always treat me as if I am a baby, but I have become so big. Just like Father."

"No, kid. You are still small and we need to take care of you," said the mother.

"No, Mother, I have grown up. Now I want to be on my own," argued the kid.

"It is not easy to live alone," said his mother, but the kid would not agree.

That evening when all the goats started walking home, the kid stayed back.

But as the night began to set in, the kid started feeling afraid. He thought, "Mother was right. I am still small. I should have listened to her. Now it's dark and I am feeling scared. There is no one here to help me."

The kid got even more scared when he saw a wolf walking towards him.

The wolf came near and said, "Be ready kid, I have come to eat you."

The kid said, “Yes, Mr. Wolf. I am ready. Please eat me.”

The wolf came nearer and the kid said, “You are going to kill me anyway. Can you do something for me?”

“What is it?” asked the wolf.

“My mother told me once that you always play your flute before you kill someone. I would love to hear it,” said the kid.

The wolf said, “Of course.”

The wolf started playing his flute. The flock of goats heard the tune and knew that it was the tune that the wolf played before killing someone.

They started checking if all of them were present and then the mother shouted, “My kid is not here.” All of them ran towards the sound of the flute.

When the wolf saw so many goats with big horns coming towards him he got scared. He knew that he could not fight so many goats. So to save his skin, he ran away.

The kid ran to his mother and said, "Mother, I am sorry that I stayed back and did not obey you."

"I will pardon you kid because you have been very clever," said his mother, hugging her kid lovingly.

THE PUFFING FROG

A frog said, "I am the strongest and the biggest."

A small frog said, "No, Uncle Froggy, you are neither the biggest nor the strongest."

"How can you say that?" said the annoyed frog.

"I went to the river and I saw a huge giant drinking water. He was so big and mighty," said the small frog.

The small frog had actually seen a big ox who had come to the pond to drink water.

"Just look at me. Can anyone be bigger than me?" asked the frog.

"Yes, he was bigger than you. You are very small. That giant was big, handsome and strong," said the small frog.

The frog did not like the small frog praising anyone else. He thought that he was the best.

"Is he this big?" asked the frog puffing up his chest.

The small frog looked at him and started laughing. He said, "You can never become as big as that wonderful animal."

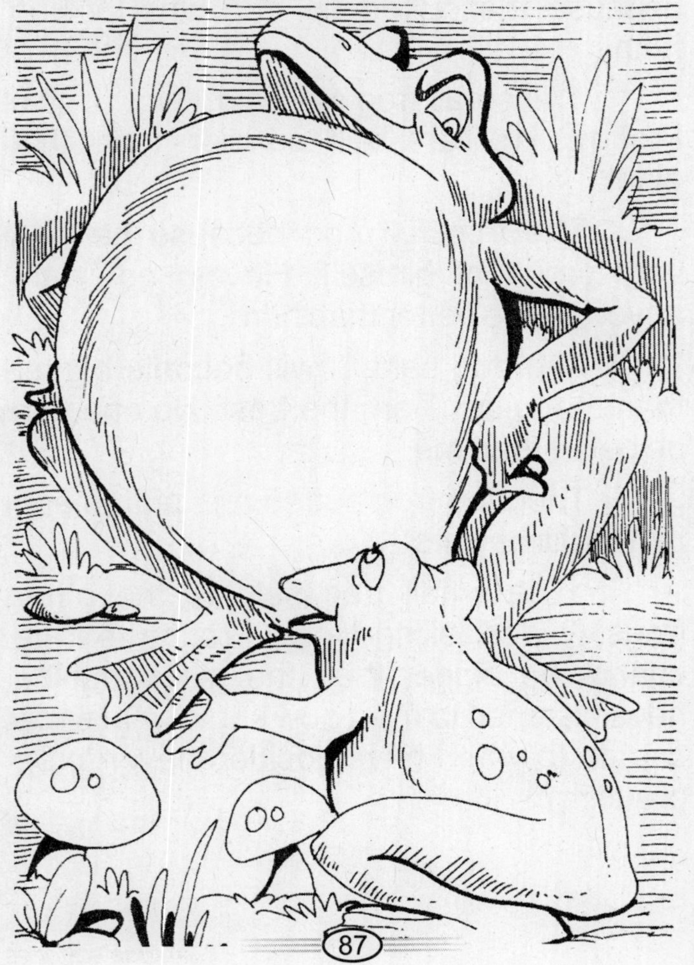

"Stop laughing. I can become bigger," said the frog and he puffed himself some more.

The other frogs had now come to see what was happening. They all laughed because the puffed up frog was looking funny.

The small frog still said, "No, Uncle Froggy, you are still smaller than that giant."

The frog felt bad because he was very proud of himself. He did not want anyone to be better than him.

The frog said, "I will become bigger than that giant. I am the best. No one can be better than me."

Then the frog puffed and puffed and puffed, till he burst.

The small frog said to the other frogs, "I was telling Uncle Froggy that he cannot be bigger than the giant, but he never listened to me. I now know what pride can do to you. I have decided never to be proud in my life."

THE FOREVER BARKING DOG

There was a dog who was always angry. All the time he either ate and slept or kept barking at others. He was very selfish too and did not care for others. He just did what he wanted.

One day he had eaten a lot and felt very sleepy. He walked around but it was very hot outside.

So the dog went into the shed which had hay kept for the cows.

The cows were not there because they were working in the fields.

The dog slept in the shed for a long time. In the evening, the cows came back.

They shouted, "Moo, moo, wake up doggy."

But the dog would not wake up. Both the cows started shouting angrily, "Mooo, mooo. Go away, let us rest and eat the hay."

The dog woke up. He saw two cows standing outside the shed. The dog felt angry at being disturbed and started barking, "Bow wow. I will not go from here. Bow wow."

"We were working in the field. We are tired. You go from here and let us eat," said a cow.

"I am tired too, so I will not go from here," said the dog.

The cows kept asking the dog to leave but he would not budge. He kept barking at them.

The other cow said, “You don’t eat hay, so let us enter and you go away.”

“I will not move from here,” said the naughty dog.

The two cows felt angry with the dog. They were tired and the continuous barking of the dog made their head pain.

When they saw that the dog would not move, one cow said to the other, “Let us shout and call our master.”

Both the cows started bellowing, “Moo, mooo, moooo.”

They went on shouting for a long time and then their master heard them. The master came with a stick. When he saw the dog barking at the two cows, he hit him with the stick.

The dog stopped barking and ran away from the shed. Then the two cows ate their food and went to sleep.

THE TWO MICE

"Oh! How nice to see you," said the mouse to his cousin brother who lived in a city.

The city mouse said, "Yes, I came here because I thought I should come and meet you. Nothing seems to have changed here. It is still so boring."

"You wash up and I will cook dinner," said the country mouse.

When the city mouse was ready, the village mouse served dinner. He had cooked roots and wheat.

The city mouse said, "Oh! Is that all you eat? How can I eat such simple things?"

"This is all that I have," said the country mouse sadly.

"Oh! no. I cannot possibly eat all this," the city mouse persisted and made faces.

The country mouse said, "Listen brother, I have nothing else here. So please eat."

The city mouse ate very little and said, "I cannot eat more of this simple meal. I am fond of eating pastries and cakes, you know."

The country mouse said, "Oh! I don't know what these things are. I have never gone to the city in my life."

"The city is beautiful," boasted the city mouse and he started telling his cousin how wonderful it was in the city.

When the city mouse had finished telling him all about the city, the country mouse said, "You must be having a very interesting life."

"Yes. Why don't you come with me and see for yourself?" said the city mouse.

The country mouse agreed and he happily went with his cousin to the city.

"Oh! It is wonderful. How big everything is! How many cars! How lucky that you see all this everyday," said the country mouse.

The city mouse felt very proud of being in the city. He took his cousin to the house in which he lived.

"Do you live in such a big house?" asked the country mouse.

"Yes, I cannot sleep like you in the open fields," said the city mouse pompously.

“Where is your kitchen?” asked the country mouse.

“You don’t worry. Wash up and then we will eat,” said the city mouse.

When the country mouse was ready, the city mouse took him to a huge dining table.

He said, “Here. All these pastries and cakes are for us.”

The country mouse said, "But someone has already eaten here. These are just the left overs."

"So what? See how many delicious things are kept here for us," said the city mouse.

The country mouse sat down to eat and the city mouse said, "Hurry up. Start eating."

"Why should I hurry? We should always eat our food slowly and enjoy every bite of it," said the confused country mouse.

"Not here in the city. Here we do everything very fast. Now eat quickly," ordered the city mouse.

They were just about to start when they heard, "Meeaaow. Meeaow."

The country mouse looked very surprised.

He said, "A cat is our enemy. Why do you let a cat live here?"

"Run," screamed the city mouse pulling his cousin with him. They ran away.

"Why is a cat living in your house?" asked the country mouse again.

"Hush. Quiet or she might eat us up," said the city mouse.

The cat ran towards them again and the two mice had to run really fast.

The cat got tired of chasing them and went away. When they saw that the cat had gone, the city mouse said, “Come on. Now it is safe. Let us eat quickly before anyone comes.”

He pulled his cousin and they again climbed the table. They sat down to eat.

They had barely put a bite in their mouths, when the door opened and the city mouse again shouted, “Run.”

Both the mice ran down the table. This time some people had come. They were the servants who had come to clear the table.

The country mouse asked his cousin, “Why are they taking away our dinner?”

“Hushhh! Shhh! The dog has come in also,” said the city mouse.

The dog sniffed and barked loud, “Bow wow. There are mice here. I can smell them.”

The dog looked around and saw the two mice. He said to himself, “I shall have a yummy mice meal today.”

The dog ran after the two mice and both ran around the room to save their lives.

A servant said, "Here doggy. Take a bone and stop barking."

The dog ran away and the city mouse said, "Thank God we are safe."

The country mouse looked angry and said, "Now there is no dinner on the table. They have taken away everything."

The city mouse said, "Don't worry. We will get something to eat from the kitchen. We just have to wait till the servants sleep."

"No thank you. I will not wait. I have had enough," said the country mouse.

"What do you mean?" asked the city mouse.

"You did not like the simple food that I served you at my house. But at least that food was fresh and not a leftover," said the country mouse.

"But you get to eat pastries and cakes only in the city," persisted the city mouse.

"I don't want to risk my life for pastries and cakes. There is no peace here. You can't even sit and eat your meal in peace," said the country mouse.

The city mouse felt ashamed. The country mouse said, “For me simple life and food is better. At least I can live in peace in the countryside.”

The country mouse picked up his umbrella and bag and bid farewell to his city cousin. Then he walked out of the house to go back to his country house.

CAN MONEY BUY EVERYTHING?

A king was very just and kind to all his people. But his son, the prince, was selfish.

The prince also thought that money was the most important thing in life.

One day the king said, "Money is not the most important thing, my dear son."

"It is the most important thing, My Lord," argued the prince.

"You cannot buy joys like love and happiness with money," said the king.

"I think money can buy everything, My Lord," said the prince adamantly.

"You have to prove that money is the most important thing in the world," said the king finally.

"I will. Let me go out and I will show you that I will do well everywhere because I have money," replied the arrogant prince.

So the prince left his palace to prove that money was the most important thing in the world.

He took with him his horse and a lot of money.

"How long will you take to prove this?" asked the king just as the prince got ready to leave.

"I will need a month," said the prince.

"We will wait for you," said the king as the prince rode off.

The prince loved his freedom. He was alone and free to do what he wanted with the money he had.

He went on riding and kept thinking of what he would do with the money.

Suddenly he realised that it had become very dark. When the prince looked around, he saw that he was in the middle of a dense forest.

He had been so lost thinking that he had not seen where he was going.

He tried to go back, but he soon realised that he had lost his way. He seemed to be going deeper and deeper into the forest.

He was very tired and he saw that the horse was tired too.

He could not see any shop anywhere. He could not even find a pond where the horse could drink water. Too tired to go any further, he tied the horse to a tree and sat down under another tree.

The Prince was exhausted. He was also feeling hungry and thirsty.

He had so much money with him, but he could not eat anything because there was no shop there from where he could buy food.

It had become so dark that he could not make out if there were fruits on the trees.

He did not sleep that night. Insects and mosquitoes troubled him. The roar of a lion scared him.

Then he started thinking. At that time, all the money in the world could not help him in any way.

He could not get food or water, nor could he feel better though he had plentiful of money.

Then he realised that what his father had said was indeed true. Money was not everything.

Money can never buy joy, happiness and contentment. He thought of his father and mother who loved him a lot.

Thinking of all this, he dozed off. He woke up in the morning to the bright sunlight falling on his face.

The prince mounted his horse and soon found the way back to the palace.

The first thing he did on reaching the palace was to go to his father, the king.

His surprised father said, “You said that you would take one month, but you have come back in one day.”

The prince said, “My Lord, it took me only one miserable night to learn a lesson and to understand that you were right.”

The king asked, “How did you learn this lesson?”

The prince told him all that had happened and how money had not helped him in the forest.

The prince said, “You were right. Money is not everything. I had so much money but I remained hungry and thirsty.”

The king smiled and then the prince said, “I also realised then how wonderful love is.”

“What do you mean?” asked the king.

"Father, you and Mother love me so much. You make sure that I get what my heart desires. I missed you both a lot. Now I know that both of you are more precious to me than all the money in the world," said the prince.

The king and queen felt happy and embraced him lovingly.

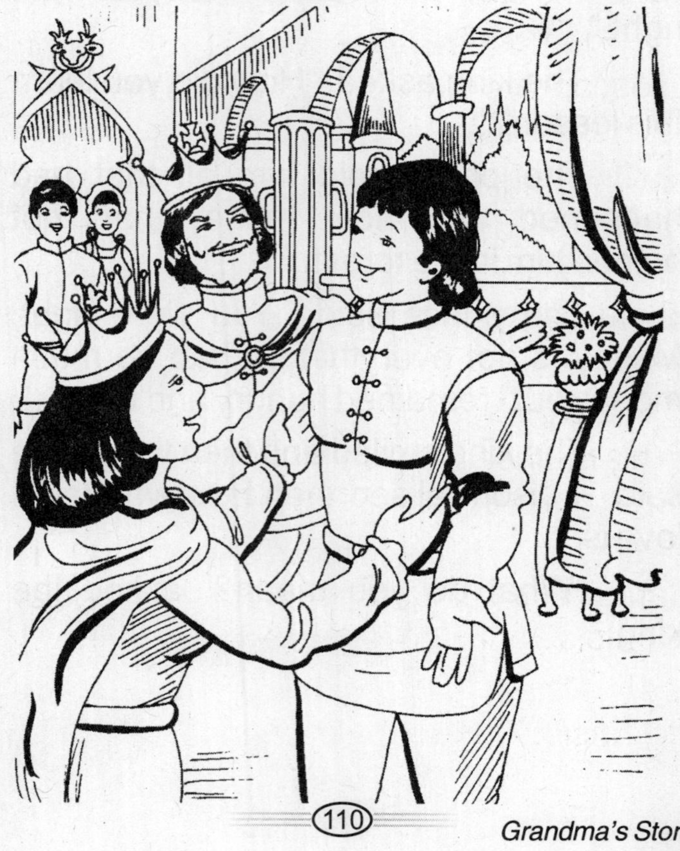

BELL THE CAT

There was a cat who was really big and strong. It was always running after mice and ate up many of them.

The mice were very afraid because whenever they went out of their holes, the cat would chase them.

Only some mice were lucky enough to escape from the cat.

So all the mice were worried. They sat in their holes all day because they were afraid of the cat.

Often they had to remain hungry because they couldn't go out to collect food.

Then one day, a small mouse said to his mother, "I am very hungry. Let me go out to get food."

The mother mouse said, "It is dangerous going out of our hole. The cat is outside and might eat us."

"There is no food in our hole. Let me go," insisted the baby mouse.

"But dear child, the cat is big, strong and very cruel. It will eat you. Don't go out," said the mother mouse.

The small mouse suddenly ran out of the hole and soon the big cat was chasing the tiny mouse.

The baby mouse ran quickly up an electric wire and climbed onto the curtain. He hid himself there.

The cat stood looking at the mouse because it could not climb the curtain. It sat down there waiting for the baby mouse.

The mother mouse wanted to save her baby, but the cat was sitting right under the curtain.

The baby mouse kept holding the curtain as hard as it could. He sat there trembling with fear. Then the mother mouse could not bear it any longer.

She ran towards the cat but just then a servant came and said, "Tom, come and drink milk."

The cat quickly ran to drink milk and the mother mouse shouted to her baby, "Run home."

The baby mouse ran down the curtain and they both rushed into their hole.

Then the mother mouse shouted to all the mice, "Chu Choo Chooo. The cat is troubling all of us and we must do something about it soon."

"I want to have a meeting within five minutes," she added.

While the cat was drinking milk, all the mice ran into the hole of the mother mouse.

Then they all sat down and discussed the serious matter.

The mother mouse said, "If the cat had not been given milk, he could have killed my baby. Please do something."

Another mouse said, "We cannot live like this. We are afraid all the time that the cat will kill us."

"Yes, we must do something soon," said the mother mouse and all of them nodded.

They thought and thought but could not come up with any ideas because the cat was too strong, big and cruel for them.

Then a mouse said, "I wish we could get the cat to go away from here, but we can't."

Another mouse said, "But we can do something that warns us that the cat is coming. Then we can run away."

The baby mouse then said, "Yes, that is a good idea. Let us tie a bell on the neck of the cat."

Another small mouse said, "Yes, then we can hear the cat coming."

An old, wise cat then said, “But who will bell the cat?”

No mouse was ready to bell the cat. They then left their holes and went into another house to live.

THE SOUR GRAPES

A fox was very hungry and was looking for food. Then he saw bunches of grapes on a tree.

The grapes looked very juicy and sweet and the fox really wanted to eat them.

But the grapes were too high for the fox. He jumped. Then he walked away and then came back running to jump up.

But he could not reach the grapes. No matter how hard he tried, he did not get a single grape.

When the fox got tired, he sat down and then he felt that all the grapes were laughing at him.

"Don't you dare laugh at me," shouted the fox. Then he jumped again and tired to get to the grapes. But he couldn't.

The fox felt very foolish when a crow said, "Foxy, you have been trying so hard but you have not been able to get even one grape."

"Oh! I was just doing jumping exercises. I don't want these grapes because they all must be sour," said the fox, as he walked away while the crow burst out laughing.

THE BOY AND THE WOLF

A boy used to look after a flock of sheep when they were grazing in a big field near a forest.

His master had told the boy, “If you ever see a wolf, you must call the villagers otherwise the wolf might kill my sheep.”

One day the boy was sitting and getting bored, so he thought that he would have some fun.

He started shouting, “Wolf! Help! Wolf!”

At once the villagers ran from their fields and rushed to help the boy.

They came and shouted, “Where is the wolf?”

The boy just laughed at them saying, “See, I fooled you all.”

The villagers became very angry and went back.

After half an hour the boy shouted loudly again, “ Wolf! Help!”

Again the villagers, armed with wooden sticks, came to help the boy and again he laughed at them.

The villagers felt very angry and scolded the boy. They warned him not to do this again.

After some days, the same boy was with his sheep in a field near the forest.

He suddenly saw a wolf hiding behind a tree. The boy felt afraid and he shouted, "Wolf! Help! Wolf!"

The villagers heard him but nobody came for his help, thinking that he was trying to fool them again. The helpless boy was too scared to fight the wolf. The wolf attacked a sheep and dragged it into the forest.

When the boy went back to his master with the sheep, his master saw a sheep missing.

Then the boy told him what had happened. The master asked the villagers and they told the master that the boy had fooled them twice.

The master got so angry that he slapped the boy hard for being so naughty. The boy never made fun of anyone after that. He had learnt his lesson well.

MONKEY GAMES

A prince went to a forest to hunt animals but lost his way.

He rode for many hours but he could not find the way back to his palace.

Tired and hungry, he sat down under a tree. He did not have water with him and he felt very thirsty.

He was so hungry that he prayed, "Oh God! Please give me something to eat. I am really very hungry."

Suddenly a peanut fell in his hands. He said in wonder, "Oh God! You do listen to prayers."

He ate the peanut. Suddenly he heard a noise from above the tree under which he was sitting.

He saw a big monkey. In a flash of a second, the monkey jumped down in front of him and said, "Give me my peanut."

"Oh! Did that peanut belong to you?" asked the prince.

"Yes, give it to me," said the monkey.

"I can't give it back because I have eaten it," said the prince.

"I don't know anything. Just give the peanut back to me," said the monkey.

"I can't give it, you stupid monkey because I have eaten it. If you want money you can take it," said the prince angrily.

"Money will not fill my stomach. I want the peanut," said the monkey.

"All right. Come with me and I will buy a peanut and give it to you," said the prince.

The monkey agreed. Then he said, "I will sit on the horse. You will have to walk."

"What do you mean? I am a prince," said the prince.

"Otherwise give me my peanut, Princy," said the monkey.

Then the prince let the monkey sit on the horse. He walked along the horse, hoping to find a peanut vendor.

He saw a man walking towards them. The prince thought that he would ask the man if he knew of some place from where he could buy peanuts.

But just then the monkey snatched the man's stick and the poor man got scared and ran off.

"What are you doing? Why have you taken the man's stick? This is wrong," said the prince.

"You keep quiet till you give me my peanut," said the monkey.

The prince was surprised even more when the monkey again leapt on another man and snatched something from his hand.

"What have you taken from this man now?" asked the annoyed prince.

"I do what I want. He had a piece of meat. Now you hold the meat, Princy," said the monkey.

"This is a very big piece of meat. You don't eat meat, then why have you taken it?" asked the surprised prince.

"Hey Princy! Keep quiet," ordered the naughty monkey.

After that the prince kept quiet and said nothing.

The monkey made the prince hold the stick and the piece of meat. The prince was fed up. He wanted to be free of the monkey.

He then saw a house behind some trees. He thought that he would get a peanut from the house and give it to the monkey and be rid of him.

The prince led the horse towards the house.

When the prince knocked at the door, a very beautiful girl opened the door. But she looked very scared.

"Please go away," said the girl in a frightened voice.

The prince said, "Just give me one peanut for this monkey and I will go away."

"You don't understand. This is dangerous for you. A giant lives here. He will eat you," said the girl.

Just then they heard a loud voice saying, "I hope that food is ready for me."

"Quick. Run up the stairs," said the girl.

The prince and the monkey ran up the stairs quickly to the attic and hid under some sacks.

From the attic they could clearly see the main sitting area of the house.

The prince was terrified to see a huge giant come in, shouting in his loud voice, "If my dinner isn't ready then I will eat you up. I don't eat you, you stupid girl, because you cook good food for me."

The scared girl said, "Dinner is ready. Please come and eat it."

And the giant ate ten loaves of bread, twelve eggs, four chickens, a big pot full of rice and drank three buckets of milk.

The monkey said, "What a lot he is eating! I want some food too. I am feeling hungry."

"I am feeling hungry too but we must keep quiet or the giant will eat us," said the prince.

Just then the giant roared, "You stupid girl, why aren't there any bananas for me?"

Then the giant hit the girl hard. She fell down and the monkey said, "I am going to teach this giant a lesson. He is too rude and cruel."

The monkey saw a bucketful of rain water. Before the prince could say anything, the monkey threw all the water on the giant.

As soon as the water fell on his head, the giant roared, "Who threw this water? Who is there?"

The monkey said in a loud voice, "Who are you, stupid?"

The giant said, "I am the mighty giant."

The monkey said, "I am the king of giants. I am very strong."

The giant said, "I don't believe it."

The monkey shouted, "This is my tongue," and he threw the big piece of meat at the giant.

The giant saw the big piece of meat and said , "Oh! He must be a huge giant to have such a tongue. He must be stronger than me."

The prince said to the monkey, "Stop it, otherwise the giant will kill us."

"Hey Princy! Big and huge people can too get afraid. But I am not afraid of anyone. Just watch me now," said the monkey as he shouted in a louder voice, "Here is my finger, just one finger."

He threw the thick bamboo stick right on the head of the giant who got so frightened that he ran away, never to come back.

The monkey jumped with joy, "See. I made the giant run away. Prince, do you like the girl?"

The prince nodded as they walked down and the girl said, "Thank you, monkey dear. This giant had kidnapped me from my palace. I am a princess."

"This man with me is a prince and now I want you both to get married to each other," said the monkey.

"But I want to get rid of this monkey. Princess, can you give me a peanut? This monkey will go when I give him one," said the prince.

"No. I never wanted the peanut in the first place. Come on, Princy. I like you both. I will show you the way out of this forest, then you both can go to your palace. I will always be there when you need my help," the monkey smiled.

The prince and the princess thanked the monkey and left for their palace.

HELP YOURSELF

A farmer had gone to the market to sell his vegetables. He was riding his horse cart back to his village.

It was raining heavily and the roads were flooded with water. The horse cart was moving very slowly.

The farmer was angry that he was getting wet and it was difficult to control the horse too.

He wanted to reach home quickly, so he made the horse run fast and the poor horse had to pull very hard.

Then one of the wheels of the cart got stuck in the mud by the side of the road.

The farmer felt very angry. He shouted at the horse, “Why did you go where there was so much mud, you stupid horse?”

He then sat down by the road, wondering what to do. He hoped that someone would pass by soon and help him out. He waited and waited.

"Oh God! Why do all the troubles come to me only? Lord come and help me. How will I reach home? I am wet, thirsty and hungry. Oh help me God," said the farmer.

Suddenly God appeared and said calmly, "You are not the only one who has troubles. Everyone suffers."

"God, the wheel of my cart is stuck in the mud," said the farmer.

"Yes, I know and I can see that you are doing nothing about it. You are just asking for my help but I will not help you till you help yourself," said God.

"What should I do?" asked the farmer.

"Just standing and looking at the cart will not get the wheel out. Shouting at your poor horse is not going to help either. Try to solve your problem," said God.

The farmer started trying to get the wheel out. He put his shoulder under the cart and tried to lift the wheel all the while pushing it with his hands.

The stuck wheel moved a little. The farmer pushed more and then the wheel moved more.

Then the farmer lifted the wheel and pushed it forward. The wheel came out of the mud. His cart could now move.

The farmer was overjoyed. His efforts had paid off. He knelt down in front of God.

He said, "Thanks for helping me, God. Thank you also for teaching me that I should get out of my problems myself by working and trying hard."

God smiled and disappeared.

GOD COMES TO EAT

Once a priest lived on his farm which was far away from the village and the city.

No one wanted to come to stay there because it was very lonely there, except a servant called Dumbo.

The priest was tired of Dumbo because whatever Dumbo did, caused some or the other loss to the farm.

When the priest asked him to see that birds did not eat up his crops, Dumbo started shouting, "These are all God's crops and grains. Eat all you want, dear birds."

So the priest had to work on his farm himself because Dumbo would make mistakes all the time. Every time the priest asked him to do something, he would make mistakes and cause some or the other loss.

The priest would work and then spend his time in praying to God. Once the priest wanted to go on a pilgrimage to a holy place.

Many other priests were going in a group and he did not want to miss the chance. He knew that he would be away for a long time.

The priest was worried about his small temple and his goats and cows. He had no choice but to leave Dumbo behind to look after everything.

Before going, the priest said, "Dumbo, don't forget to feed God before eating yourself."

The priest had stored sufficient food in the store so that Dumbo could cook everyday.

The priest went away and Dumbo started working on the farm. Everything was going on well in the farm.

Dumbo cooked food and he served food for God and put the plate in front of the image of God.

Dumbo then said, "Now, God. My master has said that I should not eat till I feed you. Come here and eat."

But God did not come. Dumbo waited for a full day, then prepared food again the second day.

Still God did not come to eat so Dumbo did not eat.

On the fifth day, Dumbo said, "God, you look after everyone, then why do you want me to die of hunger? I have to obey my master. I will not eat till you come and eat your food."

So God came and ate His dinner because He did not want Dumbo to die because of Him.

This went on everyday till the priest came back to his farm. The priest was happy that it had been a good journey for him.

But he was afraid that Dumbo might have spoilt things at the farm.

The priest started checking on everything and found that very few grains were left in the store.

Then he shouted, “Dumbo. How much have you eaten? You have finished everything I stored.”

“But master I cooked for God and myself. So the grains have finished,” said Dumbo.

“Did God come and eat all this?” asked the priest.

Dumbo said, “Yes, master. He started eating on the fifth day and he has been eating every day since then.”

“What rubbish are you talking? How can God come here to eat,” said the priest.

“But he did,” said Dumbo tearfully.

"Do you think I am such a fool that I will believe that God came and ate here," said the priest. He scolded Dumbo a lot.

Poor Dumbo turned to the image of God and said, “You are seeing my master scolding me, but you are doing nothing.”

“What will God do when you have eaten up all the foodstuff,” said the priest.

Dumbo continued speaking with tears in his eyes, “God, everyday you have eaten. But now you are not even telling him that you came to eat. You are just watching him scold me.”

God laughed at the simplicity of Dumbo and He came there to show the priest that Dumbo was telling the truth.

As God went away, the priest fell at the feet of Dumbo and said, “You have done what I could not do with all my prayers all these years.”

“But I am telling the truth. God came to eat,” said Dumbo.

The priest said, “I believe you, Dumbo and thank you. Because of you I have seen God.”

And that day onwards, the priest did not scold Dumbo. The priest brought him up as his own son.

DESTINED TO BE RICH

The king was talking to all his four daughters. He asked them, "Tell me, because of whom do you live this wonderful life full of riches?"

The three elder daughters said, "Because of you, Our Lord."

"What about you, young one?" asked the king.

The youngest daughter said, "I have got this life of comfort because of my luck, not because of you, My Lord."

The king became very angry and shouted, "What do you mean? I spend lavishly on you and you say it is not because of me that you are living so well."

The princess said, "If I am destined to live a rich life, I will be rich wherever I am."

"Do you really think so? Then try it out. Get out from here. Let me see what a rich life you live after this," shouted the king angrily.

The young princess walked out of the palace. An old maid came running to her and said, "I will come with you."

The princess said, "But I have no money to give you. I don't even know how I will manage to get food. I do not want you to suffer because of me. Please go back to the palace and don't worry. I shall be fine."

"I don't need money. I have been looking after you ever since you were a baby and being with you is a reward enough," said the maid lovingly.

"You are very kind. You know that since my mother died, I have always thought of you as a mother," said the princess. The maid kissed her forehead lovingly and they left the palace, not knowing where their luck would take them.

The maid said, "Aren't you afraid, Princess?"

"No. I have faith in God. So why should I feel afraid? He will do what is best for me," said the princess.

"You are very brave," said the maid.

"Maybe, but I am hungry. Why couldn't Father turn me out after I had my lunch?" said the princess and burst out laughing.

"How can you laugh when you have so many problems in front of you?" asked the maid.

"Worrying will not help. Let God worry for me," said the princess smilingly.

They walked on and the road led to a forest. The princess said, "Isn't it beautiful here? The open air, the blue sky, the wonderful trees. I could never roam like this when I was in the palace. Oh, I am so happy!"

But soon she shouted, "Ooooooooooooh!" The princess had tripped and fallen into a pond full of muddy water.

The princess got up covered with wet mud. Then she bowed and asked the maid, “Am I not looking beautiful?”

The maid burst out laughing and said, “Yes, you are looking most beautiful, Your Highness.”

Just then a prince and his soldiers came running. They thought that a wild animal had fallen into the pond. They got a large cage to the pond to capture the animal.

Then they saw the maid standing near the hole. As they turned to look at the pond, they were surprised to see a beautiful girl in it and not any animal!

The prince said, “Never in my life have I seen such a beautiful wild animal. Who are you?”

The princess and the maid also started laughing. Then the prince helped the princess to come out of the pond.

He took both of them to his palace and everyone stared at the dirty princess covered with mud.

The princess was taken to a room and she had a bath. She brushed her hair and wore the beautiful clothes given by the prince.

When she came out of the room, the prince was waiting for her. He just kept looking at her.

He said, "You are beautiful."

She said, "No, I think I was looking more beautiful when I was covered with mud."

The prince said, "But what were you doing in the forest?"

"I was ordered out of my palace by my father," said the princess.

"You seem to be very happy about it. Any other person would have been crying," said the prince.

As they sat down to eat, the princess told him the whole story and the prince said, "I am sorry that you fell in the pond."

"But I am not sorry. If I had not fallen into the pond, I would not be having such a wonderful dinner here," said the princess.

"You are really brave. I have fallen in love with you. Will you marry me?" asked the prince.

"You are very kind and I will marry you if you promise not to capture innocent animals," said the princess. The prince agreed to her condition.

The princess then sent a man with a message to her father, "I didn't have to live a poor life even for a day after you turned me out. I am lucky and so I live a rich life even outside your palace. But I love you, Father and I would love it, if you all could come for my wedding next week with the prince whom I love a lot."

HAVE FAITH IN YOURSELF

The child said, "Mom, I am afraid. I won't sleep alone in my room at night."

The mother said, "Why are you afraid?"

"When I am alone, I feel that I cannot do anything," said the child.

The mother said, "Will you look after the baby, please? I have some work to do."

"Yes, Mom," said the child.

The child sat there looking after his baby sister. He thought, "How sweet she is! I love her a lot and so I will always look after her."

All of a sudden, the baby turned and she nearly fell off the bed.

The child held the baby and then put her back on the bed.

He turned to see his mother smiling at him. She said, "Just now you were saying that you feel afraid because you think that you cannot manage alone. But what have you done just now?"

"I saved my little sister from falling down," said the child.

The mother said, "So you can manage yourself. I trust you, child. You are a clever child and you will always do the correct thing. So you needn't be afraid."

"Mom is right. I did save my sister. I can manage," thought the child.

The mother came in with the baby's milk bottle and said, "Thank you so much child. It was nice of you to look after the baby."

"Mother, should I sleep alone tonight?" asked the child.

Mother said, "Yes, you should because every child is looked after by an angel. No child is ever alone."

"What if the angel goes to sleep?" asked the child.

Mother laughed and said, "Then a fairy will look after you."

"Oh how nice, but what if the fairy goes to sleep?" asked the child.

"Then we are there, your father and mother," said the mother.

"But Father is always busy and what if you go to sleep, Mom?"

"Then you are there to look after yourself and you are as strong as you think you are. So never give up," said the mother.

Just then a storm came. A very strong wind started blowing.

All the windows were open and mother quickly got up to shut the windows.

The child sat looking after the baby. Then the child heard his mother scream, "Aaaaahh!"

The child could not leave the baby there, so he picked up the baby and went to see what had happened to his mother.

He saw that a window pane had broken because of the strong wind.

A piece of glass had scratched his mother's forehead and blood was flowing from the wound. His mother was in pain.

The child put the baby's sheet on the ground and made the baby lie down there so that she wouldn't fall. Then he ran and got the first aid box.

He took out some cotton wool and applied an antiseptic on it and he wiped the blood from his mother's face with it.

Then he took out and put a bandaid on the cut like he had seen on the television.

The child then helped his mother to the bed. He brought the baby also and made her lie next to his mother.

Then he picked up the telephone and called his father, “Hello, Dad. Could you please come home? Mom is all right now but she is hurt. She has a cut on her forehead. Don’t worry. I have put a bandaid.”

His father said, “There is nothing to worry because you are there, my child.”

His father came soon and then he said to the child, “Oh! My dear child, you can manage so well. Weren’t you afraid when your mother got hurt?”

“No Dad because Mom told me that I can manage myself,” said the child.

“So you can, my child. I am very proud of you,” said his father.

Mother lovingly thanked her child and the child felt very happy and proud.